A fantastic toilet read for anyone with the level of chronic anxiety that causes constipation.

A Very Inappropriate Short Story Book

Noel Leon

Reviews

"There's weird millennial Sex and the absolute wrong City. But, if Carrie Bradshaw was uber-awkward, smoking hot, and hilariously honest, her stories would sound a lot like Noel…"

—Rick Schwartz: Award winning producer of *Black Swan, The Departed, Lip Sync Battle.*

"I came for the inappropriate and stayed for the Lesbian Tinder story. So relatable and so funny!… for the modern lady who does not give a fudge."

—Jade Catta-Preta: host of *The Soup* on E!

"I felt like a fly on the wall to fun, intimate secrets. It's enjoyable and informative and gives a whole new perspective on hot chicks."

— Erik Griffin: star of *Workaholics, Murder Mystery,* and *I'm Dying Up Here.*

"Noel is such a unique character that I was very curious to read about her life. Well, it's even more extreme and funny than you'd expect! And she can write too! Lots of fun to be had."

—Ben Gleib: host of *Idiot Test* on Netflix.

"Wildly outrageous yet somehow weirdly relatable. I am both open-mouthed and impressed."

—Millie Gooch: author of *The Sober Girl Society Handbook.*

Contents

Silent Meditation Retreat

I can name a few people I'd like to send on a silent meditation retreat. But I never thought I'd be one of them.

At the <u>Texan Hindu Spiritual Silent Resort</u> I'd exiled myself to for a week, there was only one rule: no talking allowed, which conflicts with my one rule, which is I never shut the fuck up. When Rumi said, "the quieter you become, the more you are able to hear," I think he was referring to the voices in my head. Meaning, I might leave this place needing a prescription for antipsychotics if it gets too loud or crowded up there. See, in all my meditation, the only "high" I'd ever achieved was elevated levels of anxiety. I could have just gone to a regular meditation center; but, I thought, with all the uninterrupted silence, I might find the fifth dimension or something.

The retreat was run by a Hindu guru, who was authentically spiritual, having studied Hinduism in India for nearly fifty years... unlike the many self-appointed gurus in LA, who have just enough cultural appropriation to make people think they know what they're talking about. They go to meditation retreats just so they can come back bragging about how "elevated" their vibes are, *bro*. There's a ton of pretty flexible psychos "astral projecting" all over what you need to do instead of that they need to move back home because they're losing it in Los Angeles. This guru had a following akin to a cult leader. I didn't expect to be brainwashed, but stayed on guard just in case. A true guru has the presence of a cult leader... or a Cross-Fit trainer.

Maybe I'd lived in LA too long, I thought as I landed in Texas, questioning the sanity that compelled me to do this. The only experience I'd ever had of Texas was from watching my friend's mom's viral ghost hunting channel. The paranormal probably isn't the best thing to think about when entering the same desolate countryside where those "hauntings" took place. Texas is one of few states that allows people to bury their family members on their property. This resort was on a massive ranch in deep country, where I'm assuming hundreds of bodies were buried. I guess that remains to be seen. *Remains.* See what I did there?

I always get kicked out of theaters while watching horror flicks. I scream so loud and at all the wrong parts. I got popcorn thrown at me when I shrieked throughout *Signs*. I get scared and scream even in movies that aren't scary, like *The Wizard of Oz*, which I'm pretty sure was also shot in Texas. They should cast me as a girl in a 90s horror movie. All they did was scream. I was born in the wrong era. I arrived at the resort during peak tornado season. Basically, I was walking right into the eye of the storm. We were all going to die there either from a tornado or going insane, haunted by ghosts or the silence.

You know that awkward silence, when there's a lull in conversation? No? Okay, I'm a pretty awkward person, so I'm very familiar. Imagine one of those moments stretched out to five days. There were so many things I wanted to say to those other guests. Like, to the soccer mom driving the baby blue Porsche: "Where do you keep sneaking off to every night?" And, to that really tall guy: "Please stop farting in yoga class." I'm glad you're relaxed, it's still gross. But I had to keep it all in, along with gas those green juices gave me. I didn't have the confidence of yoga class gas man. Never thought I'd envy him.

My body runs on bagels and Famous Amos chocolate chip cookies. So, all this healthy shit was poison. I was enraged that first day he let one rip in class,

because I'd spent the last ninety minutes clenching my butt hole, praying to every Hindu god that I didn't let one escape. And the yoga instructor said, "Very good. Let it all out. Become completely relaxed." Well, now we all had to smell it without ventilation. Holding my breath, I nearly passed out.   She shouldn't have egged him on, because then, for the rest of the week, he let it out in every class. Meanwhile, I'm still holding it in like a damn lady. What are we animals throwing out all social conventions?! What's next, running naked in the streets? It starts with an innocent fart and ends in total anarchy.

When that soccer mom finally noticed me spying on her escape the next morning, breaking the rules *again*, she whispered: "I was dying for some solid food. Do you want bananas I snuck in my luggage?" Here she was offering me her dirty bananas as hush money, when I could smell *bacon* on her breath. But I wouldn't rat her out just yet. I wanted to see if we could sweeten the pot.

Incense everywhere had me dreaming about spicy curry, or maybe I was just craving solid food. I slept fitfully, counting shadows on the walls like sheep to fall back asleep. Until, one night, I thought a shadow noticed me watching it and I

14

screamed. "I've cracked!" I thought, or maybe said aloud—I couldn't even tell at this point. Or, the Hindu ghost gods were alerting everyone that I was an imposter: "She's over here. The one who can't meditate!" Everyone's dreaming about the greater good. Meanwhile, I'm up debating ratting out that burger chick. Or maybe that was a test I'd passed. (If she'd offered me chocolate, I would've said yes.) I'm surprised no one spoke when that alarm went off. They just walked out like mummies from their caves to the guru outside. He said someone smoking weed set off the fire alarm, reminding us, "smoking of any kind is prohibited," which obviously was a coverup for him getting stoned. I'm sure he was lighting up while having an orgy with the yoga instructors. Because there's no way that level of "bliss" came from enlightenment.

Relieved to find I wasn't hearing things, I embarked on a pleasant walk around the property to clear my head. The sunrise was breathtaking. Miles of uninterrupted nature. I could see why some would want to live in Texas, not me. Because, just then, a scorpion stopped me dead in my tracks, staring me down. I froze, peeing my pants a little. A tear fell. This was it. They were going to bury me with the rest of their family and I would haunt that goddamn yoga studio forever. Does screaming count as talking? Would it be breaking the rules if I cried for help? Could anyone even hear me this far? They really should advertise *this* on the brochure: "A beautiful country escape filled with mediation, serenity, silence, farts, ghosts, and scorpions... Not for people who don't like scary movies." I started waving to that rich chick who was *still* eating in secret, now with company behind the shed. I know she saw me, but looked away. *If I make it back, I'm ratting her out to the guru...* I realize, when left to my own devices, I will create drama. It's impressive. I have really created something out of nothing. It's a talent.

I Postmate'd some gas-ex as a parting gift to the property while Ubering to the airport. Stopping for ribs on my way, I tried out my Texan accent on the server: "Hiii, Yeeehaw, I reckon I'll have…" He seemed impressed, offended, or just a bit slow. Because he stared at me for a minute before walking to the kitchen, where he probably spit in my food. I'm somehow creating issues everywhere I go. The exact opposite of the mission I was on. Maybe I'm rebellious? Or, it's just always opposite day with me. Man, I must be a nightmare to date.

It felt so good talking again, though. I almost didn't recognize my voice. Maybe that's because of the Texan accent, which I thought I'd keep for a few more days. There was something comforting about it, along with the warm ribs soaking my insides in BBQ sauce. Like starving yourself to appreciate food again or running to enjoy sitting, now that I could speak, I didn't want to stop. Even my annoyingly talkative Uber driver wanted me to shut up by the end of the trip. I gave him five stars after he asked for a "moment of silence."

Getting off the plane in LA felt like crossing enemy lines. I wreaked of meat. LA is full of Vegans, who held up their swords, stabbing me with their eyes as I entered their territory, smelling like murder. I had bbq sauce all over my face with pockets full of ribs, while eating beef jerky. I didn't care. Pretty sure I looked like a wild animal trying to blend in with humans.

Without darkness there isn't light and without silence there isn't sound. Okay, that doesn't make sense. I'm still trying to rationalize retroactively why I went to this and come up with a good takeaway for this story. Maybe it's that if someone looks deep in meditation, they're probably just asleep. And sneak your own food into a retreat just in case you need to bribe people to save you from scorpions. Turns out that woman had the right idea.

Lesbian Tinder

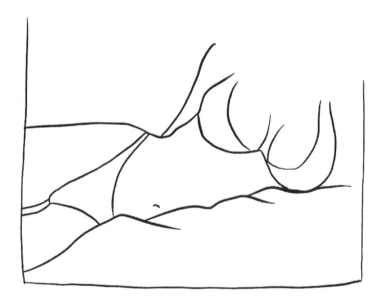

"Where is my phone?" I asked the two Doberman salivating at my feet. I must look like a snack—exactly how I got into this mess, shackled like a hound to my Tinder date's bedpost. I was in the Who the Fuck Knows Where part of Jersey... forty-five minutes outside Manhattan. Finally, I understood why people move to the middle of nowhere: to enact their weird fetishes in peace. With each house an acre apart, this neighborhood must be filled with freaks doing God knows what. It'd been five minutes or five hours, I did

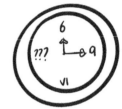

not know. Time is immeasurable in a crisis. *Had Lucy, my Tinder date, forgotten about me? She said ever so politely she was "getting water." Well, clearly I've never been more parched.* My wrist had chafed on her metallic handcuffs, bringing up PTSD from watching the movie Saw. This isn't the type of situation they teach you how to get out of in Sex Ed at the all girls Catholic school I'd attended. Just the talk of homosexuality would've sent me to straight hell, let alone fetish fornication. *If this is where I meet my maker, at least it'll be an interesting story... better than Elvis, dying on the toilet, or my gallbladder.* (That's another story for another chapter... later on.)

I recognized her parrot—Tony, yapping in the corner—from her Tinder profile pictures. I don't even want to know why he's in her sex dungeon. Cuffing a date to a bedpost with a parrot that won't shut the fuck up is a very creative way to drive them insane. And shouldn't the dogs find that parrot more appetizing than me? Unless they've had the taste of human flesh. They probably dug up bodies buried in the backyard by whatever weirdo previous occupant. And, ever since, couldn't be bothered with kibble, craving human blood like vampires. My thoughts trailed to a horny teenage Twilight nostalgia... *If vampires existed, Lucy would definitely be one. She's probably sharpening her fangs to turn me in one bite. I would love to be a vampire. People would compliment my translucent, lusciously porcelain skin, uncomfortably making jokes at dinner parties about how I never age: "This one'll look twenty-five forever. I want what she's having!"*

Eventually, I would have to move and assume a new identity when people started asking too many questions.

Tony: Momma loves you!

Me: Tony! Hey! Tony! Can you say

HELP!

Tony: Where's the goddamn remote?

Me: Remote to what? There's no TV in here!

Tony: Mamma loves you!

Me: Call your mamma!

Tony: Horseshit.

Me: Okay, that was uncalled for.

This is a position I find myself in often—hands tied behind my back, restrained, exposed—only (usually) metaphorically. It's about the time I'd phone a friend for help even though they're always absolutely useless. I can see their jaws dropping through the phone. By now, they should have realized Murphy's Law rules my life: "anything that can go wrong will."

Maybe they'd make themselves useful if I kept them on a monthly retainer. But, that might get expensive. I make a mental note to Venmo them later if I ever find my phone and caption the payment: "If I haven't sent a meme in three hours, alert the authorities." They'll know what it means. (But, that might raise some questions from other Venmo users.)

Her roommate's sudden laughter upstairs had me believing this was one sick joke. I half expected Simone (the friend I'd been out with just before meeting Lucy) to pop out: *Gotcha!* We'd been out dancing at a gay bar's "Bear Night." He'd sauntered me in with a tip of his hat, paying no mind to the beefy doorman. Even though Doormen and DJ's think they're gods in New York most don't ask Simone many questions. He's a grey haired gay fox, with an Austrian accent, an esteemed producer in the fashion industry. Meanwhile, I can't even properly dress myself. We're an odd pair. As I gyrated in a sea of jiggly bear bellies, he twirled me along to Gaga's "Just Dance." A new belly hitting me hard in the face with every turn. Sometimes I gag thinking about the particles of sweat, hair, and saliva that flew into my mouth that night. Nevertheless, despite the smell of beer and blowjobs, the atmosphere was liberating. I'll have to buy some prosthetics for a "Bear" disguise just in case I ever return solo.

Finding Simone entangled with a hunky bar boy, I made a French exit or, more accurately, a *sexit* to meet Lucy. (Note to editor: does "sexit" mean sexy exit or exit for sex?) I desperately attempted to hail a cab as each flew past, grimacing at my Joker face: mascara forming lines down my cheeks as snow and sweat melted my makeup to reveal a Halloween character. When I finally got to the twenty-four-hour vintage diner Lucy suggested, she was nowhere to be found. So, I ordered a coke and engaged in my favorite pastime: people watching. When the moon is high, the drunks and lovers tell their truths. And, oh did I overhear so many intimate details I really shouldn't have. Until Lucy's piercing blue eyes, cold yet captivating, took me aback as she finally entered. Her charcoal locks effortlessly skimmed her shoulders as she disrobed and sat. Her presence was commanding—not forced, just assertive. She hadn't even opened her mouth, and I was already eager to hear her thoughts. I hellaciously scoured my mind for a new identity, one she would find more interesting. I love meeting

22

strangers. It allows for reinvention—to be someone different… if only for a moment. I often adopt an accent at new cafes or a saucy attitude. But, I've never been much for role-play during coitus—which is why, when Lucy told me she was a dominatrix, I nearly spit out my tea. I didn't remember seeing that listed in her Tinder bio.Dating apps should require disclosing information such as this: likes long walks on the beach, smooth jazz, and ball gags.

To appear hip, I casually mention I'd been to a gay orgy once but only to observe, which didn't seem to win me any points. Yet, embarrassingly, I continued…

Me: Another time, I let a girl go down on me On My

Period! It was disgusting! The point is, she tied me up. Well, it was a hair tie. But, I'm *sooo* down with the whole S and M. BSW culture.

Lucy: BSW?

Me: Dom to tha Matrix.

Lucy: Uh, huh.

Was I down with the S and M culture? I had no idea. But, by lust or intrigue, when she finally invited me over "for a nightcap," I graciously accepted. We hopped in her Porsche and she whisked me away to what I would soon realize was the set of every horror film! I should have expected as much from her crazy eyes, a deep blue stare that drowned you. Another clue was the pitying look her gay roommate gave me as I entered, like I was one of her many prey. I could picture him condescending: "Oh…*honey*."

Lucy: Are you ready?

Me: Is there a safe word? Banana sounds fun. Why don't we use banana? She seemed amused like someone watching a cat get caught in the ball of yarn they'd just been playing with as she slowly dragged her fingernail along my wrist.

Me: Banana. Banana. Banana!

I sounded like a possessed schizophrenic with Tourettes.

Lucy: Are you allergic to latex?

Hours later, Lucy nowhere to be found, I finally screamed: *BANANA!*

Tony finally stopped yapping as the Dobermen flew to the door, hearing footsteps approach. *My moment of freedom!* I wrangled myself onto her metal bedpost, straddling it as I shoved my legs against the wall, wriggling my wrists loose until blood began to drip. Lucy entered silently, almost ghostlike, as she floated

through the room, pulling a key from her bra, and—in an act of divine intervention—finally un-cuffing me! I quickly covered my naked body, suddenly feeling even more exposed, gathering my clothes.

Lucy: Wait!

Maybe I looked back in hopes of for a redeeming moment. I still regret pausing at the door. When I say she was a sadist, I don't mean it lightly. For the next god knows however long I stayed, this chick guided me in all sorts of unspeakable acts. *Who's the dom now?* I couldn't really go through with most of them. My official moment of freedom came when she asked me to blindfold her and grab a vibrator.

Lucy: Yes. *Yes.* YES!

When I realized I was no longer needed, I tiptoed upstairs where her roommate was so kindly charging my phone. The whole situation seemed rehearsed as he gingerly handed me a bottle of water. She must have paying clients. He ushered me into my Uber: "Goodniiight!"

The Uber's repulsion to my revolting appearance was unsurprising.

Driver: Ooooh! Been there! Crazy night?

No shit, Sherlock.

Driver: You like party?

I could barely make out his thick accent, but his intentions were more than clear as he offered me his flask. Never had I ever witnessed a driver drinking straight whiskey on the job. *This must be punishment for my bad Uber rating. Is this a test? Should I call the Police?* It was three am and another thirty minutes until I would even get home. So, there was no way I was going to wait for a new ride.So, I kept quiet, praying we didn't crash and gripping the door each time he looked back. *After escaping that near death experience, I can handle a tipsy driver.*

Driver: Ha ha! I'm in the wrong lane! I can't see through this rain! Ha!

Me: Can you look at the road?!

Fuck! I'm wrong. I'm going to die. This is probably a kidnapping. I definitely fit the profile.

If someone took a photo of me then and slapped it on the nightly news, with a caption, "Female kidnapped by local Uber driver," no one would bat an eye. The nuns at my old Catholic school would warn: "See, this is what happens when you become a homosexual."

As I adjusted the rear heater, abating my impending hangover, the driver noticed my cuts from the handcuffs and a wave of misplaced concern washed over his face. He finally stopped talking and focused on the road. Never was I more relieved to have an awkward silence. (Uber must give the same painstaking conversation starter pack to all its drivers.) I wanted to silently reassure him that handcuffs, not thoughts of suicide, caused the cuts. But, telepathy isn't one of my strengths.

I drifted into a drunk slumber until he honked his horn at my destination. I bolted up, and ran into my building as he yelled through a now torrential downpour.

Driver: I hope you're okay!

He looked genuinely concerned.

Me: Thank youuu! You, too! Five stars!

Why did I say five stars? This guy should be in jail.

I've since deleted Tinder and learned (not from experience) the only way to shut an Uber driver up is holding a gun to their head and yelling, "Drive!" (I saw that in a movie once.)

A Paid Instagram

"A paid Instagram" or

"How a Covid Christmas Caught on Fire"

Uncle Dino: What's this I hear about you having a paid Instagram? I follow some girls who have that.

Me: A what?

Dino: Aunt Tina said people pay for a website.

Aunt Tina, mid-bite: Is this Vegan?

No one responds as they stop side conversations to watch my face turn a more festive red than the tacky Christmas sweater my mom insisted I wear.

Me: It's, um—

Nona, my stereotypical Italian grandma: Lorenzo!

My grandpa, Lorenzo: What?!

Nona: What's she talking about?

Grandpa, yelling over the table: A website, Maria!

My grandma's voice is ten decibels above the appropriate conversational tone. One time, as a child, I had the balls to ask finally, "Nona, why are you yelling?" "I'm not yelling it's just my voice," she replied even louder in her thick Brooklyn Italian accent. I've found the more I question, the louder she gets. See, my family's from Sicily—the bottom of the boot: the soccer ball shaped island embarrassingly attached to Italy, like that fucked up uncle we all have. The black sheep of the family, that's what Sicily is. Northerners scoff at our gaudiness and validly assume any Sicilian is connected to the mob. My grandpa said he had dead bodies dumped on his doorstep as a kid and his family had to pay people off to ensure their safety even after he and his five brothers moved to the U.S. I'm not sure if this is true, but I admit I enjoy having potential mafia ties. There's something magical about it. That's why mafia movies do so well. Nona flaunts tacky gold jewelry, which she refuses to remove, even in the shower, for fear of someone stealing it right off her. If you ask me that's the definition of "new money." Also, Italians have a hint of paranoia. They don't trust nothin', especially the banks. I'm pretty sure they have money stashed somewhere so secretive they probably even forgot where.

So, back to the Christmas table, where—like a terrible game of scrabble—I'm scrambling words in my mind, which is quickly turning to mush. I look to my boyfriend Andrew like "can I get a vowel?" as I float out of my body, witnessing my worst fears fabricate. Then, (maybe shocked by my astral projecting) he clenched my leg so hard, I'm pulled back into my almost paralyzed body. *That's a cool party trick. I should remember that for later.*

Me: Um, It's just a subscription site where I post behind-the-scenes photos and videos of comedy sketches from photoshoots for magazines.

Nona: "So what's your job?"

Nona, still uneasy with the concept of the internet (because I'm sure she doesn't trust it on some level) looks extremely worried and confused. I pretend not to hear her question as I gulp down cheesy ravioli, savoring the taste, hoping they've bought the bullshit I just sold them. But, like a no return policy, there's unfortunately no refund on that imperfectly packaged lie. My grandma lights her second skinny cigarette and takes a large puff, now blissfully disinterested in the topic. "Andrew, have you been to church?" she bellows. Andrew's Jewish and it's the middle of Covid so of course he hasn't. This is a weird passive aggressive attempt by Nona, something she's known for. Dino and I quickly whisper in unison, "Just say yes." Andrew: Of course.

Good boy. I pet his cashmere sweater.

Nona: You know, I was in the paper for bringing Jesus to the women's prison.

Andrew: Wooow.

Nona loves every opportunity to spread the Good Word. Most of her bling, from grandpas cha-ching, is Jesus paraphernalia: crosses even the most grandiose rappers would covet. They have assets in Jesus pieces. If they leave me anything, there's a good chance I'm getting a bunch of 24k gold Jesus Jewelry. I would have liked to have been a fly on a wall in that prison as she sauntered in, donning her velour Juicy jumpsuit, while preaching that placing Jesus on a pedestal in your heart prevents all problems. It's a bit of an oxymoron, but she's set in her ways. As they say, you can't teach an old Sicilian new tricks. Andrew, being from New York, is accustomed to this breed of eccentric Italians. My mom, wearing her highest heels to Christmas dinner, would blend in Jersey, he says. She mildly flirts with him at the table—outrageously inappropriate, but something I'm more than accustomed to. There aren't too many things she could do at this point that would shock me. Dressing up for family occasions in stripper shoes with her cleavage showing is the least of my concerns. Have you ever heard of "kissing cousins"? I should end it there in case she reads this. Let's just say that, to her—and, again, a certain breed of Italians—third cousins don't count. *Sicilians love keeping it in the family.*

"Leave room for Jesus," Nona retorts as I peck Andrew's cheek, whispering an apology on behalf of my family.

My mom loves to set me up with hunky guys of all ages—usually younger. So, Andrew's accustomed to texts from random dudes with varyingly chiseled abs popping up on my phone.

For Example: Hey this is _____. I met your   mom at Ralphs. She showed me your Instagram. I'm into fitness too. [Insert chiseled abs pic.]

I'm sure she was hitting on them and considers pawning them off on me an act of charitable selflessness. Or, it's probably an attempt to vicariously re-live her twenties.

My mom should never be allowed to have a pool boy. Grandpa pours another glass of the expensive limoncello I gave him, proudly sipping while taking in Tina's perfectly manicured backyard—once featured in a Home Depot commercial. Something she's happy to share with everyone she comes into contact with at least three times. It's amazing how many topics she's able to make circle back to the home depot commercial. I'm not sure her friend

Marnie's new baby has anything to do with the commercial, but Tina has a gift. Grandpa's hair color matches his unnaturally yellow drink in such a way that I chuckle under my breath. I love him to death, but I find the odd ways older people try to reclaim their youth endlessly comical. As I've always said, elderly is the time to do all the fun stuff you feared trying in youth because of that whole not wanting to die thing. When I'm eighty-two, I'm definitely

trying heroin, going skydiving, installing a sex swing… things like that. Ya know, the things normal eighty-two-year-olds do.

Recently, my grandpa and I have been writing a book about his life, called *An Immigrant Boy*. But, unfortunately, since I'm his granddaughter, he glosses over the entertainment—like mafia shit, fast cars, and drugs... We all know the millions he and his brothers made didn't come from working in that salami shop. Although, they do have some pretty good prosciut in Brooklyn.

Aunt Tina (for the second time): Is this vegan?

Grandpa: How the hell am I supposed to know?! Just eat it. When I was growing up, I never complained about the food. You know why? I was just happy to be eating.

Dino: I can't eat any of this. I'm on a program.

He winks at Andrew as if he's supposed to understand Dino's neurotic dieting rituals. Every year he says the same thing and every year it's the same ten pounds only with a different "program" he's on, that we all have to try: "You gotta get on my program." Dino stands up and farts into the closet, the combustion echoing outside as a trickle of toxic fumes seeps out. "Jesus Christ!" I exclaim.

Nona: Watch your mouth.

Me: Sorry.

I used to call Dino "Uncle Fart" because he had serious gas issues. Girls would apparently dump him because he got up so many times to use the bathroom. I don't even want to speculate the context of that statement, but I'm sure it was pretty bad. He probably has an undiagnosed stomach issue that everyone's just ignored. The type who only dates playmates and always has the perfect excuse for one girl or the other not working out, he's your archetypical "heartthrob" even into his early fifties. I guess in 2021 you would call that a "fuckboy." I know he seems too old to be a fuckboy, but if you met him you'd understand. He still has a youthful glow, and by that I mean he's stunted emotionally. I would call him a *fuckman*, but that sounds too much like a superhero. And, I don't think a fifty-something year old with flatulence who can't commit to women is considered a super hero of any kind. (Note to editor: look up the man equivalent of fuckboy in the Urban dictionary.)

To distract my family from life's hot topics, I'd purchased $400 worth of cannols from an authentic Italian bakery. How I thought that would create a diversion, I have no clue, but you know the old saying, "you can never have too many cannolis." If that isn't a saying it should be.

Canoli Distraction Technique:

Effectiveness: 5/10

Stomach Ache: 11/10

Sugar Rush: 8/10

I cradled my canols like a security blanket throughout dinner, in my arsenal for any instance of conversation redirection. I've found offering food is always a great way to divert attention. Plus, the world cannoli is just comforting. "Yeah, there're mint ones & affogatto…" "I love how small they can make them." The limit of descriptive sentences I can make about cannolis does not exist. But, on the rare instance you need a moment, just stuff one in your mouth.

Andrew says we have to go back to that bakery because they're going to roll out the red carpet after how much I spent. And, the owner, with his 70s Italian pouf hairstyle, is a historical treasure. He greets everyone who enters (who're usually Sicilian) like a long-lost cousin. They probably are. Sicily is a small island— hence the "kissing cousins" thing. See how I tied everything in? Should we jump to the end of this dinner? I promised short stories after all. Although, I do think I've held up my end of the bargain on the "inappropriate" part.

Now, maybe from the noxiousness of Dino's incessant excretions, or the combustible nature of conversation, the backyard shed poignantly exploded upon Nona igniting her third skinny cigarette, torching any hopes of a normal family dinner. "Opah!" Andrew held up his glass. At least someone's entertained.

Whitney Houston Cost Me $10

Dog Rescue Receptionist: I will always love youuuuu, Whitney Houston!

Me: She's going to an excellent home. I've kept my fish, Tony, alive. Actually, I'm not sure he's still alive. But, I'll keep *her* alive.

Noel, keep it together!

Me: Thank you!

The overly cheerful receptionist seemed a tad uneasy as I ran out with Whitney, afraid they'd change their minds.

"Act normal," I said to my friend Rob, driving the getaway car.

Rob: What? Why?

Me: They're watching us.

Rob: Noel, did you just steal this dog?

Me: Just drive.

Let's back up a beat. This might very well be *the most* white girl brunch story of all time: legendary basic white girl material. When my friend Rob casually convinced me to get a dog one day over brunch, he was not expecting having to drive me to a Rescue right after we got the check. Listen, a lot can happen over white girl brunch. Really, it's his fault. He should've known what happens at brunch, stays at brunch unless we talk about getting a dog. *Then, we get a dog!*

He tried untangling the web he'd weaved for himself, reminding me that owning a dog is basically like having a kid. What I needed to remind *him* was that it's Sunday morning and I'm drinking bottomless mimosas. Dogs and children are topics to stay away from. I hope he's learned his lesson.

Me: Today, Halloween, is a special day therefore the *perfect* day to meet my soulmate! And, I let's stop and get a dog costume.

Rob: This poor dog.

I'd like to think it was an act of divine intervention: me finding Whitney. Or, maybe she found me. If so, I'm honored to be chosen. After all, she is Whitney Houston reincarnated. *What? She is.* It was the name given by the shelter and I wouldn't change it. Yes, not only did I get a dog during Sunday *brunch*, but I got a dog named Whitney Houston who strut out of there like a diva, ready to start her new life of being waited on, hand and foot. She'd just come out of a very toxic situation (like her relationship with Bobby Brown) that landed her in the

kennel. It'd been a hard life. She'd seen things on the street that you can never unsee. Whitney Houston constantly reminds me "there *can* be miracles when you believe." Like when she hopped a six-foot fence to catch a chicken and kindly dropped it at my feet. A man bearing arms barreled out, shouting, "Who stole my motherfuckin' chicken!"

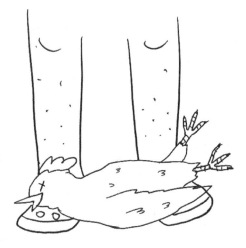

My first instinct was "Run!" Meanwhile, Whitney smiles like it was her proudest moment as the chicken's guts poured from her jowls onto my fresh, white Hitachi Nike sneakers. I almost puked. "Now this is *my* responsibility?!"

As we ran from the screaming farmer, I realized Whit and I formed our own gang: outlaws, living by our own rules, a menace to society. She's my sidekick in shenanigans we don't dare speak much like "Pete the Pup" in the Little Rascals (to whom she bears a striking resemblance)…And, that evening, over candlelight, Whit and I devoured her capture. It was very romantic.

Whitney and I are sexy co- dependent bitches with separation anxiety. On dates, guys basically watch me watching her. Meaning, I spend the entire time I leave her home alone, checking nanny cams on my phone. Then, they get to foot the bill, drive me home, and have my door slammed in their face while her and I make out. What can I say? I'm a catch. On the rare occasion they get to second base, Whitney Houston jumps on the bed, licking their balls from behind just as they ejaculate. It's very traumatic for everyone involved, except for me and Whit. I'm pretty sure this is why my ex, Alex, and I broke up. He's probably still seeing a therapist for that. The best dates I've ever been on have always been with her. Some restaurants in Venice let her sit in a chair across from me at the table. She graciously listens to me ramble as I feed her fish caviar. At least ten percent of the time, I'm seated near a friend or loose acquaintance who always reacts with concern for my mental health, which I find incredibly offensive. Sadly, society still doesn't accept public displays of our kind of love.

Sometimes, I wonder if I should get Whitney a little "nip tuck" on that extra long nipple of hers. Whichever puppy from her litter pawed its way to the top of that food chain was ravenous. But dogs have no concept of modesty. She's

unfazed, letting it all hang loose. Maybe, that nipple is her source of confidence as she mounts all the male dogs at the dog park. Or, it's like ET's finger, giving her a heightened sense of direction when it blows in the wind.

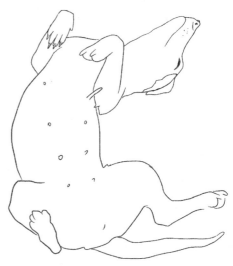

LA *would* be the one city to have a dog plastic surgeon. I wonder if it's like going to target. You enter for one thing and leave with the entire store.

Whitney and I would go in for the nipple and she'd leave looking like a different breed. I picture the surgeon having flamboyant arm gestures.

Surgeon: We could do a little lift under ze chin right here to accentuate ze jawline.

Me: Okay. Is that necessary?

Surgeon: Then we could arch ze tail like his, giving her much better posture.

Me: Okay. Wait, I have so many questions.

Surgeon: You don't have an ugly boyfriend, do you?
Me: No.

Surgeon: Do you find yourself attractive?

Me: I guess.

Surgeon: Are you a little vain

Me: I—

Surgeon: So, you would not have ze ugly dog, would you?

Me: No, I wouldn't. I mean, I don't.

I'd lean down and whisper into Whitney's ear: "Don't listen to him. You're beautiful."

Surgeon: Ze nipple is $10,000. I can throw in paw implants for $2,000—half price!

Me: Sold.

What can I say? I love a good sale. Poor Whitney. Now, I have to start a GoFundMe for the nipple.

To be honest, Whitney's swag and the way she rocks that nipple makes *me* more confident. I'm no longer worried about having old lady nipples when I'm elderly. She almost makes me want one saggy, long nipple for some street cred. It could be a new fashion trend where everyone starts stretching out their nipples. It's all about the confidence. I want her confidence. When Sarte said, "Hell is other people," I think he was talking about owners at LA dog parks: a very specific breed of crazy. If you thought Karens were bad, try spending an hour observing wanna be actors and influencers in their natural habitat, Instagramming their dogs. The episode of Animal Kingdom dedicated to "influencers in the wild" (also the name of a very popular Instagram account that proves my point) would go something like this:

Narrator: "And, here we see the bitches breaking off into cliques. A creepy male in sandals, pounces on a female, using his Husky as bait. He doesn't seem to notice the tiny poop particles collecting in his toes. But, will she? What do we have here? The breed of Apologetic Doofus, who's constantly apologizing for their out-of-control dog as they post photos of it on Instagram. Also known as the "fuckboy." And, here we have a woman exposing her buttocks to potential mates in very short shorts as her Chihuahua dry humps a Dalmatian."

One time, while Whitney was humping a male dog, an owner came up to me and said, "Like dog like mom, eh?" And, asked for my number! I gave it to him because I *do* relate, but still!

On shopping excursions, retail workers always ask what Whit "services" and I reply "she services my anxiety." Then, I go into really unnecessary detail, making them beyond uncomfortable. Hopefully, now, they won't ask anyone else such a rude question. Next time they'll think twice before having to learn about Whitney's favorite sashimi. Really, she services my anxiety by making me feel less deranged when talking to myself in public. Instead, I talk to *her* as if she's a person. I used to get so many strange looks. And, I still do, but they're different. Now, people look at me like I'm the only one who can see her. Or, maybe the listening to how cute my doggy voice is. Sometimes, I accidentally use this high pitched squeal on my barista: "Who's a good boy! Yes! I'll have a cup of cawfee! Yes, I will. Good boy!" Or, sometimes in bed: "Gooood boooooy!"

Would you believe all this love, servicing, and companionship only cost me ten dollars?! I know little about finance, but I'd say that's a pretty good return! I never thought that shelter would actually give me a dog because my desperation was palpable. My energy was almost manic, like Buddy hopped up on sugar (in that movie *Elf*). The first time Whitney Houston sat on my

lap I screamed. Then, I cried. Then I smothered her with affection. It was an emotional rollercoaster that she quickly jumped off, panting out the window probably thinking, "Who the hell is this psycho?!" I replied (debuting my doggy voice), "This psycho is your new mommy! Yes, she is!" Whitney whined, wondering how her life choices landed her in my lap. She was so malnourished that her bones protruded into my leg. And, the shelter apparently couldn't figure out why she was shitting blood. She'd been on every shelter's kill list in the Valley (the porn capital of America), tossed around like a cheap whore, that magical nipple hanging out. At $10, I knew they were trying to get rid of her which is why they let me take her home against their better judgement. Everyone cringed as I demonically screamed, "You *will* be my best friend!"

When Rob finally sped onto the 405 freeway, I finally out a sigh.

Me: That was so close!

Rob: Can you please tell me what's happening! Who's this?

Me: This is Whitney Sophia Houston, Whitney Houston *reincarnated*. Thank you. You're welcome. She's my new best friend.

Chronic Anxiety

Disclaimer: this story is purely for my street cred and there will be a lot of weed slang I've recently picked up off the Urban Dictionary. (And, according to my editor, I shouldn't use "stoner humor" whatever that means.)

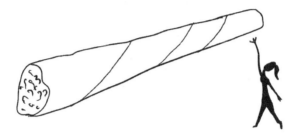

I have chronic anxiety that usually holds me back. But, sometimes it unleashes my creative brain, the neurotic parts that make me unique. In Los Angeles *everyone* thinks they're unique. To "make it" you have to be or at least tell yourself you are: "fake it until you make it." This city is full people heavily in denial probably because everyone's parents coddled them too much and told them they could all be superstars. Who knows? But, I *do* know that when you do get to hang out with an *actual* superstar, Snoopdog, you best *act* special and get on their level. And, by level, I mean if Snoop passes me the chronic you know I'm going to take a puff even though I have—like I said—*chronic* anxiety.

That skunk puts me in a funk. Not the Motown funky groovy vibe, the *Where did I put my dog? Am I saying these words out loud? Who's that talking in my mind?* kind of vibe. And, there were all types of vibes the day I smoked with Snoop.

His recording studio is what you'd expect from a living legend. There's an NBA sized basketball court, vintage arcade, and real movie theater… like a popcorn machine and everything! I needed to move in! I'll just sleep in the closet and sign over my soul on the lease. My dog can hang with Snoop (cue Snoop DOG joke) and we can all be best friends. His best friends (which I was soon going to be one of) were watching the Laker's game. But, I don't really care about basketball. So, I used the time to win over his son.

Jeff Ross, the "Roastmaster" from Comedy Central, had kindly invited me and at halftime I followed him into Snoop's studio, where he was laying down his latest track… where this is where this *very* short story begins… But, a long story if you're high, as I learned that day. I'd forgotten to Google "weed consumption etiquette." But I'm pretty sure it's like dinner with my Nonna: it's a compliment the more you consume. No-one really offered me the Chronic. So, I volunteered to hit it… one too many times. And, after constantly forgetting that I had to pee, remembering, and then not being able to move, I finally peeled myself off the chair.

Inside the bathroom I screamed, seeing double in the mirror. I was so scared my demon doppelgänger would follow me into the stall. I did the dance everyone does when they really have to pee, while loudly clearing my throat to cover up for all the screaming everyone must have heard. So, if anyone would have walked in the bathroom they would have seen me dancing, while screaming, and intentionally stopping to clear my throat. Like I was performing a weird ritual, or possessed. Maybe Snoop could have thrown it on a hot new track? These thoughts swirled through my head as I flushed the toilet, even though I still hadn't peed. I walked out, clenching my legs. Yes, I went to the bathroom to not pee.

I made eye contact with Jeff, who looked legitimately concerned. And, halfway to my seat, I realized *everyone probably thinks I didn't wash my hands.* So I went back into the bathroom, braving my demon double. Because the worst thing they were thinking was of course that I hadn't washed my hands. Usually, when hearing a ritualistic seance taking place in a bathroom and that person not even going to the bathroom, the first thing anyone thinks is: "Did she wash her hands?" Also, do demons even use soap?

When I returned, two of Jeff were staring at me, which made me doubly uncomfortable. Because, I couldn't tell which was him and which was his demon. So, I squinted really hard, making the other one go away. *But, which one went away?*

Jeff: Are you okay, Noel?

Me: Yeah, why?!

My paranoid eyes were trying to figure out if he also was seeing those ghost ninjas attacking me. They came from the shadows, carrying tiny swords, and went away every time someone walked past the light.

Jeff: Okay, just let me know when you want to go. I can drop you off on my way home.

Me: No, I'm good. Thank you.

At least, I think those words came out of my mouth. It was really hard to tell. Someone passed me the chronic again. And, I had to take another hit, not for me, but for future Noel, who would ooze street cred. *Just power through it, baby! You'll thank me when you're Snoop's best friend and he writes a song about you.*

Jeff lingered, as if waiting for me to do something. Maybe I hadn't actually replied. After that second hit, I couldn't even blink. I wasn't even sure I was breathing. *Isn't Chronic supposed to be enjoyable? His friends smoke for fun, right?*

It seemed like they were all dead, like their souls were floating in the smoke clouds above their bodies.

I'm a debaucherous person, but I'm also very Type A, which I know is a contradiction. It means when I'm extremely fucked up, I still like to have a game plan and be in control. I don't need to know where we're going, I just need to there's a destination even if it's just to get laid or blackout. It could be to get laid or to even blackout. It could be a freaking game of hopscotch. I just need to know where we're trying to get to. No one in that room seemed to have any direction. There's no way they could get any more high. It's almost like, at this point, since we're all dead (unless that was the goal) maybe we should just switch to something else or go home. The only way I knew they for sure weren't dead was the munchies. Everyone was having a snack attack, including me. But, too paranoid to move, I just sat there, salivating. I'm sure they thought I was strange, studying them chew.

I shooed those damn ninjas off my face as I tried to figure out my next move. If anyone hadn't thought I was strange before, they did now. I was redefining the term "crazy eyes." *Snoop's seen worse.* My high got higher and higher until I needed an exorcist to remove the chronic from my soul. I was near possessed. As Snoop played his next track, the look on my face was sheer terror. I needed to peel myself off that chair and gracefully exit before I offended anyone else (neither of which I was currently capable of). Thank god I didn't smoke this before my Comedy Central pitch meeting. I guess it *could* have been worse. (That's a later chapter.)

In an interview, I once heard Snoop say he won't smoke with people who talk too much. So, when he finally spoke to me, I made sure to not reply. Which I think is the wrong time to be silent, but at least he'll invite me back. I spoke in my head, or maybe out loud. I hoped if I spoke in my head loud enough, he could hear my thoughts. Maybe we're cosmically connected by the Chronic (being best friends and all).

Getting up to leave felt like the last round of a boxing match that should have been called after the first. These guys were all heavy weights champions, and I was getting knocked out left, right and center. Just getting out of my chair was a struggle. I would've stayed, but I didn't want to be *that* bitch: the last girl at a party who just looks desperate. Also, I still really had to pee.

I thought smoking weed with Snoop would forever change me, like my thoughts would all be in rap verses and I'd instantly have swag. Maybe, I'd even grow out my pubic hair and start wearing t-shirts that say "I get high on my supply." But, really, from those two hits of Chronic, I just became *chronically* anxious for days. At least I now have street cred. I'll have even more when this book comes out and the whole world discovers I've smoked with Snoop. You now can send any rap album inquiries to my manager. (The story of my rap career comes later.)

Client Cleaners Confidentiality

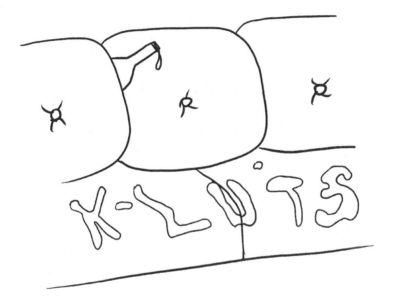

There's a small gem of a dry cleaners in Venice, California, just blocks from the beach. It's a rare find in 2021, where—especially after the pandemic—most Ma and Pa, non-chain operations had shut down. A father and son operate what looks like the set of a ninety's sitcom. Everything's old school from the cash register to the phone on the wall and signed celebrity polaroids. *I wonder if they'll take my photo. It wouldn't be horrible exposure.* Adorned with coins for good luck, a smiling Buddha greets you followed by a comfortable, musty aroma. Little did the Wang Family know I would become their best customer, bringing many new smells and entertainment, starting the fateful day where this story begins.

Our First Encounter: Wine Stains (Basic, *I know.*)

I'll twist this disgusting tale into a beautiful metaphor for not holding onto "bad vibes" or some pop psychology cliche like "unprocessed emotions always find a way of coming out." Here it was the evening of my third date with Andrew, which happened also to be my birthday (lucky him). And, my existential dread over aging direction came out in every direction as I projectile vomited cheap wine, undigested pasta, and sprinkles of edible confetti, the literal icing on the cake. At the ass-crack of dawn, feeling my imminent death approaching (*this is what old age must feel like*), I slyly stole his wine-stained couch cushions and tiptoed to the door. Never was I more grateful for my dog's melodic snores, muting my escape.

I slipped a mask over my mouth as I entered Wang's cleaners, the unbearable stench of vomit still on my breath circulating into my nostrils. Vinny Wang slowly glanced up from his morning paper (because of course he still reads the morning paper). The door chimed open to behold a spectacle, I'm sure, although nothing out of the ordinary for Venice. It's home to an eccentric breed of drug addled homeless, mis-fortuned misfits, and the "tortured artist" type: wanna be rock stars whose careers took a turn for the worst. I fit right in that morning with my puke crusted hair, looking "heroine chic:" a traditional Venice Beach boardwalk style. Didn't Kate Moss make the dehydrated look a thing in the late 80s? I can picture Barbara Walters commenting on my catwalk of shame: "She's wearing what appears to be ripped men's boxers, an oversized surfing sweater, and…to complete the look… Is that an upchuck stain still fresh on the sleeve?! Wow! The detail in this Vomitus Trainwreck outfit is unparalleled."

Praying he couldn't smell me under his mask, I cleared my throat and blurted a raspy "Hiiiii" which sounded possessed as my voice cracked two decibels higher than any sound found in nature.

Vinny: Good morning. How may I help you?
He must've thought I needed help in more ways than not and he was right.

Does he get me? This feels very intimate and, possibly the start of an interesting relationship. I'm literally giving him all of my dirty laundry up front!

Me: There are wine stains all over these cushions!

He senses my desperation.

Vinny: Ooooh.
Fuck, he's onto me.
Me: Yeah.

I held back a hiccup and began sweating profusely. Vinny: Hot outside?

Is he flirting with me?!

Me: Yeah.

Do something sexy. Maybe I can get a discount.

While twirling my hair seductively a flake of puke flicked off and we both watched as it fell to the floor. His face grew disgusted and suddenly serious like *he* was about vomit. Was this becoming one of those scenes in a movie where everyone throws up? I almost threw up as I felt that piece of pasta in my hair and heard the wet slam on the floor. He must have wanted to throw up. I saw him clenching his jaw and could sense his mouth watering. We held a stare for a second, like a standoff of two people trying not to be the first one to puke.

Vinny: I'll have it ready by three. Goodbye.

<u>Our Second Encounter: Blood & Dog Hair</u>

Vinny: Back again?

Me: You remember me!

His lack of response was off-putting. He seemed less than overjoyed at my return which was disappointing because I consider myself a pretty likable person (even in this circumstance). But, I literally saw his jaw clench and mouth watering again.

Wait, does the sight of me make this guy puke? What is it that's making me so into him now?
Me: Same couch cushions. Haha.

Vinny: Wine stains?

Me: No, I thought I'd mix it up this time. Blood and dog hair!

Vinny: Oh.

Me: Yeah, I'm a klutz.

I'm not sure klutz is the right word. When someone shows up with blood stained anything and says "I'm a klutz" they're probably covering up an accidental murder they've just committed.

Me: No, no. It's a bagel—a bagel accident

Yeah, that sounds believable.

Me: My dog always jumps on the couch. I've been training her not to. Don't worry, she's okay! It was the bagel. I was bleeding, NOT the dog. I had to get stitches, because I was distracted, holding a knife when she jumped on the couch.

I show him the stitches on my wrist of all places, which did not help the mood.

There's something about being put on the spot that always makes me feel like I'm lying even when I'm not. Maybe it's because I do things like stab myself in the wrist and then bring blood stained cushions into dry cleaners with a story involving my dog and a bagel. It's a talent, really. He was most certainly reporting me to animal control.

Vinny: I'll have it ready by three.

Me: Thanks!

The door-chime mocked me as I left. Feeling eyes on the back of my head like a sixth sense, I glanced back (which made me look even *more* suspicious) to find him watching me. But, it's Venice, I'm sure he's not phased.

Our Third Encounter: Poop

By this point in our relationship, Andrew & I hadn't had "the talk" yet. And, by "the talk" I'm mean the inevitable conversation about my irritable bowel syndrome. There's no sexy way to casually incorporate IBS into conversation. So, I chose over dinner at a Romantic Mexican restaurant, while seductively scarfing a juicy bean and cheese burrito. Discomfort and disgust washed over his face as I explained the inevitable trajectory of the evening. He was probably having a reaction to the jalapeño tacos I'd forced on him.

Lucky for him, my explosive diarrhea wouldn't come until the next morning post coitus and coffee, while jogging around his block. I wish I was making this up for a low-brow poop joke. But, I'm not that desperate. You already bought the book. Isn't the biggest joke that an Instagram Model wrote a book?… *moving on…*

Or rather, *not* moving on… Because, I mid-jog on this bright and chipper morning I froze, feeling something wet drip down my Lululemons. There was no stopping it. This had to be karmic retribution for that time I ran out of poop bags three years ago and left my dog's shit on a lawn. I bargained with the universe as I tiptoed inch by inch back to his house:

If he's still surfing when I return, I will never ever eat bacon again. I will go on a hunger strike. I will rescue baby cows from slaughter. Is that what you want god of bean burritos?! Name it and I will do it!!! Pleeeease, just do me this one solid!

(Solid… see what I did there? This whole chapter is just one long drawn out failed poop joke. You're welcome.) I opened the front door ever so slowly, not making a peep until I realized no one was home. *Thank you!!!* I sat down and stretched. I'd address my eternal debt to the universe later. *I'm sure the whole rescuing cows thing is negotiable.* Whitney judgingly sniffed what I instantly realized were poop covered couch cushions. *Fuuuuudge!*

Vinny: And, how may I help you today?

He lowered his paper.

Vinny: Oh…It's you!

They should really work on their welcome.

Me: We have a bit of a situation.

Vinny: Do *we?*

He seemed unsurprised. *What was that look? He's a dry cleaner, it's his job to handle "situations." Although, three in one week… I'd probably think I was being punk'd by this point, too.*

I approached the counter and realized I was wearing the same outfit as before: very old boxers and a grimy ripped sweater. *He must think I don't own any other clothes. Or, maybe he thinks I'm a Steve Jobs type who only owns one outfit for efficiency. Or,* probably he didn't realize because he was clearly avoiding eye contact, except an occasional glance to sus out the situation.

He recoiled as I handed him the bag. It seems he's taking this personally. I responded with a gave him a look that said "My dog ate my homework and shit on my couch," or something to that effect.

Communication is all in the eyes. But, if you have crazy eyes, no one can ever tell what's up with you, like all those drifters in Venice. I have no idea what their eyes are trying to tell. I sensed that he probably thinks I'm planning to murder as I'd been staring at him for way too long and quickly looked away. He's officially gone from suspicious to scared.

Vinny: It'll be ready at three.

Me: Thanks!

A VERY INAPPROPRIATE SHORT STORY BOOK

That's going to cost me extra.

Our Fourth Encounter: Bleach

After being so so sick of Wang's missed placed judgments, I took matters into my own hands when I got *this last* stain on Andrew's couch. I'll jump to before the stain because this needs a little explanation. See, there are chickens living in Venice. They roam around this middle school by my house and my dog loves to chase them. Okay, you get the picture. There was a lot of clucking. *RIP, Fred.* I named him out of respect. He probably had a good life. Now, I'd learned after the first time Whitney caught a chicken that it's too disgusting to try and pry it out of her mouth.

"She needs a trainer!" were Andrew's first words when we got back and Fred— somehow still alive—fell out of Whitney's mouth. He clucked. It was a miracle.

Me: Fred's alive!

Whitney leapt to catch Fred, ramming him into the couch, blood and feathers exploding. There would be no socially acceptable way to explain this to the cleaners. So, I grabbed bleach from under the sink and squirted it haphazardly over the massacre.

Andrew: WHAT ARE YOU DOING!

It felt like a crime was committed and PETA was surely on the case.

Me: I'm gonna... I'm gonna go to the cleaners.

Andrew: Yeah.

He ushered me outside with the cushions, definitely questioning his sanity for dating me.

This time, Vinny dropped his paper as I sulked in covered in sweat, bleach and chicken bits. I could see the blood draining from his face as he reluctantly

excepted the cushions. The shame in my eyes made this feel like a very illicit exchange.

Wang: You know that if I suspect foul play, I will report it.

Me: Isn't there some sort of cleaners client confidentiality?

Wang: You mean attorney client privilege? *No*.

50/50

"Please, God, don't let anyone go through my phone" was my first thought when I had a near death experience. So, clear your phone history before you die. Actually, just do it right now. Trust me. If I wasn't about to die, my search history would have had me committed: Can my dog hear my thoughts? What is the average size of a human nipple? How do I know my Postmates aren't stalking me? If that's not enough, the thousands of nudes—close-ups of all my pimples (sent to my unlucky doctor), and weird angles of my body—would do it. My second thought was, "Of course I'm dying right now, only the greats die young," which was a testament to my ego at nineteen years old—that I believed this when I hadn't accomplished *anything* yet.

My gallbladder decided to be a party pooper one Friday night, bursting my fun, infecting my blood, putting my body into septic shock. Most people die instantly. The nurse, wheeling me into emergency surgery, said I had a fifty-fifty chance of surviving. A coin toss is always fifty-fifty or drawing a black card from a fifty-two card deck. I guess in poker those would be some pretty good odds. I just never thought I'd have to place a bet on my own life. And, if I've learned anything, it's that the house always wins.

I'd hoped to have a near death experience worth bragging about, like spinning through a portal into another dimension or meeting Elvis in Heaven. Reddit is full of people boasting that they've seen the afterlife, or had brain orgasms while self-resurrecting. I do feel blessed to still be alive, but also seriously gypped. And, after opening me up so intimately, the hospital could have given me a souvenir. Like, a t-shirt that says, "I had my gallbladder removed, and all I got was this lousy scar." Wearing that around might garner some weird looks.

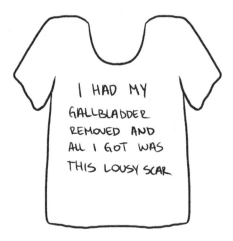

Also, I'm a huge klutz. So, there are a million and one more interesting ways I could've tragically passed than from a gallbladder. I guess that's life, though. You don't really get to pick and choose who gets to have a famous death.

Perhaps the fates had spared my life for me to find love. Because, I was sent the Intensive Care Unit: a romantic heaven for a hypochondriac. Like a cat with nine lives, I was now on the prowl. Surely, I would find love with a hot doctor, who could give me an orgasm while diagnosing all my ailments, the best form of multitasking: "When we were in doggy position, what did you think of that mole on my back?"

My only competition was those gossiping nurses who I was forced to eavesdrop on because I couldn't go anywhere with tubes hooked up to me. It was that or watch Telenovelas. I don't even speak Spanish. So, I would make up funny lines for the actors and laugh at my own jokes. The nurses thought I was insane and maybe I was. Who knows? Crazy people are *always* the last informed. Everyone's too polite to tell them they've gone off their rockers.

I didn't see *any* hot doctors on my floor. So, I made a mental note to explore other levels when I was discharged and finally invited my boyfriend to visit. *I guess he'll do.* Oh, was I a sight to behold. I must have looked and smelt like a homeless clown. Because, I'd painted makeup on my face, which had ballooned to twice its size from all the IV's and hadn't showered in almost *two weeks*. I know this the point in a relationship when you're supposed to be vulnerable. But, the morphine told me to seduce him, instead. I tried to make out with him so aggressively, one tube disconnected from my arm and he respectfully pushed me away. The nurse came in to fix my IV, breaking all the sexual tension, which apparently was only in my head because he later told me I was *hilarious*. I'm pretty sure hilarious is not the response anyone wants when turning on the charm. But, we dated for four years after that. So, I guess some of my desperation must have been attractive. Or, he took pity. But, probably, there's something seriously wrong with him.

Even dying from some sort of freak sex accident with my boyfriend in that ICU would have been more exciting than my gallbladder bursting. At least I could have been famous from being featured in that show "Sex Sent Me to the ER." I'm not sure why the ER is making talk so much about sex. I guess I have this

69

expectation of going to the hospital and leaving with a husband. Be careful what you wish for.

A few years later, I ended up in the ER from jogging straight into a pole in Central Park while texting. This was not my proudest moment, but a better story than the gallbladder. I had a really hot doctor this time. I flirted with him while blood gushed from my brain. I was seeing double: two hot doctors, almost like a threesome! He didn't appear aroused by my concussed state. I guess a damsel in distress didn't do it for him, or my overwhelming body odor mixed with blood and tears. Maybe, he thought running into poles was a red flag. But, doctors are so chivalrous, he probably just didn't want to take advantage of anyone in such an altered state of mind. I wrote my number on my bedsheet before I left and am still waiting for that call. Those nurses were probably jealous and threw it away. It's on my to do list to get another injury in Central Park so I can see him again.

Most people develop a new appreciation for life after a brush with death. I developed *that* and a more severe form of hypochondria. After realizing my own body could destroy me, WebMD became my best friend. Now, I go to the ER at the slightest hint of constipation. Most recently, I went for a mosquito bite, thinking I had West Nile Virus. But, going to the ER for every little thing does have a perk: I increase my odds of finding love with each visit! After WebMD'ing all my ailments, I map out which hospitals have the hottest doctors... It's only a matter if time.

This isn't a self-help book, but in this chapter I did give some solid advice. If just one person is inspired from my story of beating those 50/50 odds of living or finds true love in their local ER then this book is a success!

The Day the Internet Thought I Was Dead

Being a hypochondriac, I was assured the day would come sooner rather than later... *the day the internet thought I was dead*. I pictured all the hilarious ways I could untimely pass and how my followers would react, contemplating conspiracies. My art would surely be left under appreciated—unlike Picasso or those rappers, who got their big breaks in the afterlife... living it up, sipping champagne in Heaven. There should be a disclaimer when entering the internet: WARNING, this substance is highly addictive. May cause obsessive thoughts and delusions of grandeur when used compulsively. Aka, put your phone down, you Instagram fien!

From the moment I decided to "ghost" social media, I constantly checked all corners of the internet, looking for people wondering where I'd gone. It felt like stalking an ex's Instagram from a fake account after blocking them. This might seem like I staged my own funeral just to see how people would react. But this really was an attempt at personal growth... at least initially. Ross, in that ninety's sitcom, Friends, pathetically pretends to be dead and listens to his high school crush gushing about him at his own memorial. It's hilarious, but now, way too relatable. Let's be honest, we'd all like to be a fly on the wall of our funerals and a social media disappearance is the closest thing to it.

During the pandemic, I posted on social media non-stop—so much that I felt out of touch with reality (more than usual). I felt like I needed to get to know myself again...to go frolic in nature and do all that shit you see in tampon commercials. Self proclaimed "gurus" on Instagram, post so many self-help memes and all that meditation hippie shit non stop. There's no way they have any time at all to practice it. So, I decided I'd do something radical: disconnect from the internet for three months to give the whole living thing a try. Now, I

74

couldn't go anywhere or see my friends because it was still a pandemic. But, according to those "gurus" all I needed was to look inside. I could leave my environment by elevating my mind, astral projecting, and become my own best friend through getting to know my inner child. That last part was questionable because some have said that I'm a bit childish. What would probably be more helpful would be getting to know *future* Noel, the more mature version of me, who has her shit together.

At first it was rough. Stopping drinking wasn't even this hard. I substituted the instant validation of likes from my followers with licks from my dog. She is a diva, but loves treats. So, I bribed her to give me love. The level of attention she received during those three months was borderline dog abuse.

Things felt very slow, like I was suddenly experiencing life at half speed. I almost questioned my sanity because it felt so surreal. I realized the internet was just a vortex set to hyper-speed, programming your brain to fifteen second bursts of attention. And, actively debated (with the voices in my head) whether "going off the grid" was leading me into insanity. If I *did* actually lose my mind it's not like there would be anyone around to point it out. I lived completely alone and my dog refuses to communicate properly. So, it's not she'd say anything.

If someone suspects something wonky's going on in their brain, they should be able to put a sign on telephone posts (like people have for missing pets), "Missing: My Mind," along with a picture of what they looked like before they'd gone insane. "If found please call 123-456-7890. Reward: Restoring the public's peace."

As days went on and calls didn't come flooding in from sleepless followers distraught over my disappearance, I began to worry no one even noticed. I sat by my phone like a fifty's house wife, building resentment. *I thought we had something good going on. What could they be doing that's more entertaining than clicking on my posts? Really though? Why haven't they alerted the authorities?*

ZZZ ...

An influencer who just STOPS posting. That's worse than a child goes missing in the park. The possibilities are endless for me. Don't you realize, the moment I'm not attention seeking, I'm obviously most attention seeking? I'm beginning to spiral.

I wanted to talk to them about this, but of course I couldn't post. So, I began many of my followers on Instagram. It's really hard when you have a million, but not as hard as you'd think especially when you have all the time in the world. I know this was supposed to be a digital detox, but my curiosity got the best of me. *As long as I don't post I still can go on to social media for some sleuthing.* By the way, this is *way* unhealthier than just posting.

Ugh! Life was sooo much easier when I just cared about people caring about me, instead of now caring about why don't care about me.

Voila! My detective work paid off... Drumroll, please... I discovered Reddit forums igniting rumors of my kidnapping and sooo many other exciting things! This was way better than watching Netflix. (There is a limit to how long you can watch a gay tiger wrangler.)

<u>Trigger Warning:</u> This story is about to get mad dark. So, put the book down and hug your dog. Or skip ahead to the next chapter...

The speculations on Reddit about my whereabouts made me realize death was lurking around every corner. Validation from all these Reddit posts became a double-edged sword. I literally thought people were out to get me, like I was important enough to be assassinated. Don't get me wrong, I was honored to have conspiracies dedicated to me, but nearly peeing my pants at the slightest provocation.

I needed a distraction from my distractions at this point. I needed a digital detox now from my digital detox. This wasn't going very well. And, I'd gotten to "know myself" enough to seriously get on my own nerves. So, I took up a few hobbies (other than Reddit), which you can steal if you're trying to better yourself as well:

1. Buy a drill. Drill holes in walls. Then, feel like a badass lesbian.

2. Buy shelves to cover holes. Mount shelves. Question if the amount of shelves you now have on your walls makes you look crazy.

3.   Buy something to put on shelves.. The internet says plants grow better if you talk to them… Great! *I can give my dog a break from hearing my thoughts!*

4.   Enjoy your plants: blast music while having stimulating (although one-sided) conversations. (Pinterest says large ferns prefer classical.) Realize your neighbors are way too nosy and order curtains.

5.   Buy pretty pots for the plants, so they feel special. Then, go down an Amazon rabbit hole, ordering more useless shit…like things for an apocalypse… Or, stuff that's so weird it's almost kitschy. Ya know, just to give Jeff Bezos your money.

6.   Finally clean out that messy closet and fill it with *new* useless crap. Call it your "Amazon Closet," vowing to return everything. But you never do and it just piles up.

7.   Then, accept the life of a hoarder and rent a storage unit.

In all seriousness, when the apocalypse *does* come, I'm not letting any of you in my storage unit bunker after all the jokes you've made about it. (You know who you are.)

Now, this last hobby is a bit different. And, by different, I mean I'm embarrassed to say it out loud (so, thank god I'm only writing it for the whole world to read). I suppose we all have weird quirks... Okay, so, here it is... I got soooo antsy, I started printing photos of ideas for things I wanted to post on Instagram. Basically, I made a mock up Instagram on a wall in my living room. I taped them up then stood back and looked at them, giving them mental likes. I wanted to see what it felt like to follow myself, on my wall, in my bedroom. Okay, I'm guessing this is when you unfollow me on Instagram, thinking "What the hell is she talking about?" Honestly, I don't know...

Oh, I forgot to mention some of the conversations I had with my plants during this digital detox...in case you were wondering, which I'm sure you were: *If I think a funny thought but I don't post it, am I even funny? If I don't brag about my six-pack on the internet, what's the point of working out? Who knows? Nobody knows. Because nobody knows.* I think I actually witnessed a plant wilt.

Finally, after a transformative three months of self-discovery, posted on Instagram. I felt like Tom Hanks in "Castaway:" I had grown chin hairs, my plants were Wilson(s). I had a renewed zest for life. Yes, nothing bad *actually* happened to me, but just knowing that people thought something had been such an ordeal which is why I wrote this memoir. You can never make one too soon. I also wrote a will and took out a life insurance policy (like j-lo did on her legs). You never know...

Thank you for following me. If I followed you back don't be creeped out. I'm still stalking some of you. And, to who it may concern: I'm leaving everything to my dog, Whitney Houston, for her to finish her singing career...

My Rap Career & Dave Chappell

I've now spent years mourning the end of my rap career, which was painfully short-lived on account of my inability to rap. I could have been one of the greats. My songs would have been about actually funny things, not "bitches" and "hoes." (The only "bitch" I'd mention is my beloved dog.) I would've changed the game. The only funny rap song people really know is "Dick in a Box" by Justin Timberlake, a parody… My rap songs would be funny, but not a joke!

Everything I know about rapping I've learned from that "Rapper Wives" episode of the "E! True Hollywood Story," which was so much more entertaining than educational. Also, I've Googled "How to Rap," because that's what the internet is for, right? Anyone can be anything thanks to Google.

Me: How do I rap?

The Internet: Repeat words that rhyme really fast.

Me: But, like what if I say it a little slower?

Internet: Like a retarded person?

Me: No, like poetry. (P.S. That word is offensive.)

Internet: By who? Your mom?

Me: You need to learn some manners and then use those manners to find a job so you can move out of your mamma's basement.

Internet: Ooooh, nice burn.

Me: Is there anyone else in this chartroom who can teach me how to rap? Or, am I going to have to rap battle this punk for some chatroom cred.

It's all about the cred.

My rap career began and ended with Dave Chappelle, when I decided to rap on stage at the Comedy Store one night. It was a "Roastbattle," when comics hilariously roast each other on stage. There's always a pronounced winner of each battle. But, that day no one won. Because, they would be forever haunted by the emissions from my mouth. Unfortunately, my rap voice does sound like a demon escaping my body. It's disturbing and uncomfortable to watch, or so I've been told. (I can't bring myself to watch the videos). I could almost hear the other comics shaking their heads. One approached me after: Do you ever rehearse things in your head before speaking them out loud? Me: I try not to.

He thinks he's sooo funny. The only person whose opinion truly mattered to me that night was Dave Chappell's. If I'd spit Grammy gold, I'm sure I would be famous now. Instead, Chappell sat next to me and grabbed my mic to save me from myself, or maybe take control of the crowd.

At least I acted like a legit rapper. I pulled up to the comedy store in an Uber SUV. (But, not an Uber black. Let's not get crazy.) I brought an entourage because I remembered on VH1's "Behind the Music," rappers always roll with their ten best friends. I didn't have more than like two friends really, but I did have a lot of loose acquaintances. So, I sent last minute e-vites to every single one of my Facebook friends. *Is this how E! True Hollywood stories begin?*

Chappell was such a draw that everyone showed up, which I found a little upsetting because most of them had ghosted my previous dinner invites. And, the Comedy Store manager wasn't impressed when I told him I was going to rap on stage so he should "make room for my entourage." I guess he just doesn't appreciate the culture. I'm sure if Kanye brought h*is* entourage, they'd get seats right up front, which is what I told him when I bribed him to let them stand in the back. I don't think he heard me, because he just walked away. Also, yes, I'm now at Kanyes level in my head, standing with a few of my Facebook invites who'd ditched my dinner plans.

Now, anyone can be a famous rapper on TikTok by repeating the same vowel over and over. I think they say "eet" or "skert." White boys are getting billions of views filming in their parents' basements without ever having to learn the rest of the alphabet. But, before TikTok, we had to actually come up with lyrics. So, I'd invited my friend Danny for a writing sesh an hour before I was going to go on.

Danny got stoned while I got drunk, you know, to get the creative juices flowing… we were a powerful combo. See, he's one of those friends who's down for anything and has your back even when he shouldn't: a typical "Yes man," something every entourage has. *Yes* men are crucial in the celebrity culture. They're good for your ego and horrible for your career.

We thought we were so funny. I almost peed my pants, laughing at lines we never wrote down. Truthfully, they might not have been that funny, but no one will ever know. Because, the words that came out of my mouth on stage weren't the ones we'd rehearsed and actually weren't even in the English dictionary. Danny pretended not to know me during my performance, in traditional *Yes* man fashion. When the going gets tough, the Yes gets going (or gets too stoned to pay attention).

Really, I don't remember why I decided to start a rap career. I think it's from watching too many illogical Disney movies that make you believed you could do anything. Instead, I should have Googled how to avoid public embarrassment. The internet would have told me to stay the fuck home. Or, maybe I thought I could rap from playing with Barbies: girls learn style is more important than substance. They get bullied if they don't dress their Barbie right, meanwhile little boys are picking fights and learning consequences. I blame Barbies and Disney Movies for my failed rap career.

My shrink once said I have the female equivalent of Peter Pan Syndrome: when adults refuse to grow up. Los Angeles is a mecca for this. Also, I don't really blame Barbies. I need to stop laying blame, this might be part of my problem. I've somehow just blamed Disney for me not being able to rap.

I definitely looked like a rapper or a pop star, with eyeliner to my ears that a toddler would paint. My cleavage hung so low, the Comedy Store should have charged extra for the show my nipples were putting on. They each made at least one or two appearances. *Cardi B's got nothing on this.* Women in the audience disowned me for mis-representing my gender (as the only female on stage that night). My performance was offensive in so many ways, especially when I developed a Jamaican accent. I still can't replicate it. The whole thing must have been some form of cultural appropriation.

I know you're dying to hear these lyrics, but my editor said, "Please, don't!" However, in this book I'm an open book. So, here's the only verse I remember:

Yo my dogs, my dog is Whitney Houston. That's her name. She takes me to a Higher Love. That's also the name of her song. We Almost Have it All. That's another song name…And, here's the chorus…

(Feel free to TikTok it and if you become a famous rapper, you're welcome. Don't tag me.)

I pointed to the manager, who was giving me the look of death. People are strange. It's so hard to tell what's on their minds. He was probably upset he hadn't thought to infuse rap with comedy, thinking, "How can anyone top this?" (Isn't it that if you don't know what someone's thinking, you should convince yourself what you want them to be thinking?)

It's actually better that no one clapped, that no one fed the beast. Because, if they had, I'd most likely devoted myself to a (delusional) life of rap. And, there's no way I'd make it in the music industry. It's just way too political.

When everyone booed, I pulled out some prosciut and sat down. I'm Italian, so it's normal to stress eat cured meats. (Yes, I keep an emergency stash in my purse. It also comes in handy on first dates, at bad restaurants, or when Uber drivers ask you uncomfortable questions.) I accidentally rubbed my eyes while eating the meat and now looked like a ravenous raccoon. After the booing stopped, I remember putting the mic between my hands in prayer position and bowing. I saw that in Kanye's "I am a God" music video. I didn't exactly feel like a god, but I did want to bless the occasion like when a priest anoints the Eucharist at a Catholic mass. I blessed the audience after serving mad skill.

My rap ended when I began singing a duet with Chappell. Really, everyone was singing, but in my head it was just me and him, harmonizing. Half the audience had already walked out. I think rest stayed because they couldn't look away from the train wreck I was orchestrating. Chappell had grabbed from me when the booing began. He diverted attention, singing "That Thing" by Lauren hill, while the piano man played.

Some say that when I sing a demon hurls all sex appeal from my body. Apparently, I exorcise my attractiveness to birth to a monster. I want to take this moment to officially apologize to everyone whose ears I've permanently scarred. People say the Comedy Store is haunted by legends who've graced its stages. If it's not, I'm pretty sure they're now rolling in their graves after the spectacle I made on their sacred stage. Thank you to the audience member who said my voice "can be used as a torture method in prisons." Nice of you to volunteer this information.

"Never again will I go on stage at the comedy store drunk," I told Danny afterwards at a twenty-four-hour Thai joint down the street. "Fran Lebowitz

says you can't make the same mistake twice. Because, then, you don't have an excuse."

Danny: What is that? What are you doing with your face?

I was still exaggerating expressions like I'd done during my performance. "YouTube said rappers are very expressive," I garbled in between delicious gulps of soapy wet noodles.

Me: And... my face is stuck like this.

Danny: Don't do that.

I drowned my shame in soup as I slowly sobered up. Never was I more grateful for hot liquids, warming my insides, making me feel cozy and comfortable again. The world can be a very harsh critic. I think that's why 24 hour Thai restaurants were invented.

I went on stage drunk one...two...or three more times, but who's keeping count. I didn't rap so I could at least use a different excuse for bombing. I think the moral of this story is to always keep it fresh, mix it up: don't make the same *exact* mistake twice. And, don't choose Roastbattle (with Dave Chappell) to debut your rap career, because you *will* get roasted.

A Good Person

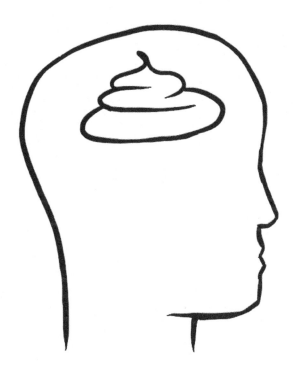

I see therapy as a test of my brain like when you get an ear exam in school, secretly hoping you'll hear you have such exceptional hearing, they're giving you the day off and an award. Or, when you get a physical, wishing someone would say you have some sort of genetic abnormality, possessing untapped superhuman abilities. Everyone does this, right? I guess these are kind of obscure examples, but I'm weird. When I see a therapist, I'm looking for validation that I am a genuinely amazing, nay superior human being. That sounds incredibly narcissistic and grandiose, and also all the wrong reasons to get therapy, which is exactly why I'm in therapy. Oh, I save humility for the PhD's.

My dad says, "It's counterproductive to feign normalcy during these sessions." At which point I counter, "Are you calling me insane?"

Dad: No, I'm saying you should tell her what's really going on.

Me: That the voices are talking to me?!

Dad: Nevermind.

There's no right answer to that question. And, although the voices haven't reached out, yet. There are a few, you know, generic things, like seasonal depression and debilitating anxiety, I probably should address. I'm sure by this point, some of you have gotten to know some of those voices. Yay, now we're all friends. Instead, I get into character, playing the part of someone who regularly showers. I lather on effortless glam (a makeup look that takes hours to achieve), hoping I'll pass for an innocent well rested baby, not a sleepless hypochondriac. Then, I slip on leather Sperry loafers, a token item in the closet of anyone "adulting," and, a cashmere sweater along with my most expensive jeans (the kind hipster boutiques pull from hobos and charge $300 for) to scream "fuck you money" despite what my bank balance says. (I never listen to my balance. She's always so negative. I prefer positivity.) I hope my therapist doesn't see through it at all. I'm just being natural. *Just. Act. Natural.*

This act is well rehearsed as I've used it a million times. Well, almost a million. Whatever number of therapists follow me on Instagram. Therapist shopping is like shopping for a prostitute. Once you've gotten your rocks off once or twice, it's time for something new. And, there's nothing like that first high. (I would think. I've never gotten a prostitute. Although, I have gotten offers. But, it stops there.) I elicit their empathy with a spiel about a tortured childhood, bringing it home with how well adjusted I've become. Applause, appraise, and astonishment are welcome/expected at this point in *The Noel Show*. And, what follows is usually:

Therapist: So, what brings you in today?
Me: Well…

I lay into a self-deprecating monologue that highlights my strengths. Like, in a job interview, when you say your biggest flaw is obsessive cleanliness. I make sure to never so much as hint at my demons in front of this trained professional who would surely have me committed. My deepest secrets are hidden on sticky notes scattered throughout my house. "Epiphanies" or a "manifesto" depending on how and why they're discovered.

Six months into sobriety, I was so nervous to go on a first date with that guy, Andrew, that I relapsed. I got black out drunk and invited him inside, forgetting about the sticky notes. I even can't imagine how he reacted. And, I don't remember. I was drunk. A drunk girl inviting a guy up for a sultry occasion only to find psychotic ramblings plastered all over her walls, like every serial killer has. He should have run. Instead, he said the notes were "endearing." It must have read like graffiti that drunks scribble in bar bathroom stalls or like a really strange puzzle. He was hoping to decipher it, to finding a hidden clue one day that would make it all make sense. Because, why else would someone leave something like that up for public viewing? (But, he never found the clue and ultimately gave up.)

My editor just asked what the point of this chapter was and I told him to mind his own business. Then, he said "this is what you're paying me for!" and that he needs "proof of the sticky notes to better understand this chapter." Let's just say, after I show someone these notes they can't run and they can't hide… just ask Andrew, during the visiting hours I've implemented for him.

Would it be narcissistic to assume therapists in the greater Los Angeles area discuss me in reverence amongst their inner circle? I'm sure there are meetings they all go to, where they just rant and commiserate about their patients like AA meetings but for shrinks: self help for the self-helpers. Sometimes, I console myself by picturing all my therapists sitting in a room, agreeing that I am in fact A Good Person. I know there's patient confidentiality, but let me have my fantasy. This is my Pornhub: a bunch of therapists talking about me in a circle.

Can I get a Life Line?

Me: It's a show about a show.

Exec: Okay.

Me: They're here. They're there. They're doing things with people who come and then they go. Ya know?

Exec: No.

Me: I mean... it's soooo *not* a show that it's actually a pretty good show.

I was definitely taking liberties with whole eccentric writer thing at this Comedy Central pitch meeting. The three network execs, two male and one female, seem perplexed probably because there's no LA cliche they could my fit kind of crazy into...which I guess makes me an original. Hoping this chick was a lesbian, I'd worn a (now pit-stained) rainbow t-shirt under my pantsuit, and was not so subtly attempting to flirt. I was trying too hard at all the wrong things. Rainbow t-shirt, CHECK. Actual show idea... not so much. Although, they did seem impressed by how explosively I was bombing. Maybe I should've leaned into this whole Andy Kaufman pitch I had going on. Instead, I basically tried to pitch Seinfeld the way George Costanza pitched Seinfeld on the show Seinfeld. Which, I'm sure has been done both intentionally and unintentionally several times over the last few decades. I'm not even pitching Seinfeld the way Larry David actually pitched. I'm pitching it as if I just copied George Costanza on the actual episode:

Seinfeld: Well, what's the show about?

George: It's about nothing.

Seinfeld: No story?

George: Nah, forget the story.

I'd honestly rather be the best at being the absolute worst than remotely mediocre at anything, which is what I'd convinced myself. Basically, if there was an Academy award for worst pitch, I would have graciously accepted. I'd coerced three of my most responsible friends to come as lifelines. Because, for some reason, I saw this meeting playing out like a game of Jeopardy meets Who Wants to be a Millionaire, thinking I'd get to "phone a friend." "Congratulations! Your prize is....." The wheel spins past my options: public humiliation, a Comedy Central swag bag, an IG shout out... And, it lands on: "Your own TV show!" Confetti falls from the air. In my fantasy spin in slow motion through pools of confetti, making eye contact with each camera man as the audience applauds my mere existence. Oprah struts onto set, "You get a show! You get a show! You get a show!" pointing to each of my friends.

Exec: Did you have a presentation or something?

Suddenly, I hiccup so loudly I startle myself out of this daydream. As the smell of bourbon wafts from my mouth, I can tell everyone's finally realizing I'm drunk, which suddenly makes me painfully aware of how drunk I actually am.

Now that I'm (permanently) sober I can gracefully explain this retired signature move of mine: self-sabotaging by getting fucked up before important situations. I'd snuck into the bathroom just a few moments prior to ruin this opportunity, drowning my nerves in shots of bourbon and snorting some Adderall. The only other option I'd even considered was setting off the fire alarm, which seemed a tad excessive. In hindsight, anything to get me out of that meeting would have been better than actually following through in that state.

My "lifelines" were absolutely useless, wishing they'd read the fine print before signing up for humiliation by association. Lifeline number one, Paul Eliah, is a successful comedian. Alex Zeldin is a comedy writer. And, Ian, my third in line, is in investment banking. So, they all had much better things to do. Paul always looks unbearably happy when he's extremely uncomfortable, making him my go to cheerleader. Throughout my pitch, his smile was nearly to his ears. Ian, on the other hand, definitely had a stroke. Someone really should have called the paramedics. He didn't blink once. And Alex, although responsive, kept rudely nudging his chair away from me. I don't entirely remember how the rest of the pitch went down, but I should have stuck to that Seinfeld schtick. Because, just when my performance couldn't get any more painful to watch, it did.

Me: We have celebrities. And, they walk into the kitchen, like Kramer

(Now, I'm *literally* making Seinfeld references)

Me: or a really annoying relative... They walk right past the hosts as they—

I stopped mid-sentence, pulling the Snickers I'd stolen from Reception out of my pocket, dumping them on the desk, shoving the least smooshed ones in my mouth and continued.

Me: It's a show within a show. It's scripted, but unscripted.

How Poetic.

Female Exec: No.
The lesbian exec was not having it as a chunk of chocolate flung onto her notepad. I paused, loudly sucking caramel from my front tooth. Those shots I'd taken were definitely kicking in. The extremely tall exec (they really should've worn name tags) looked like he wanted to film this for some sort of Instagram meme. At least he was entertained. I think entertained is the word I would use.

Tall Exec: So, it's a talk show?

I blatantly ignored his question to text Alex under the table: *What"'s going on?* His face turned beat red as his phone buzzed and he nudged me to look at the lady who was staring at me. "She's like obsessed with me," I said in (what I thought was) a whisper. I should have closed the pitch with, "And, scene." So, they would've hired me on the spot for my excellent method acting abilities. Then, that meeting would have ended with a standing ovation.

Basically I'd just asked them if they wanted to lose a bunch of money while (unintentionally) seeming to not give *any* fucks. And, it's crucially important to appear like you give at least one, maybe two fucks when asking networks for money. Because, even though Hollywood does get off on "creatives" acting like they're too cool for school, they ultimately want to make a profit. Hopefully, they were at least entertained by how little fucks I appeared to give or maybe just by how unaware I was. Unaware and not giving a fuck goes hand in hand, right? Either they thought my words held a hidden genius they were too left-minded to grasp. Or, they thought I most definitely had blown someone to get this meeting and were wondering who. Maybe they'd just let me go on with pitch while waiting for security to arrive. *That's how confusing my pitch was.*

Me: Oh! Did I mention they sit in between a few ferns during the interview segment?

As no one responded, I questioned whether I'd even said that out loud.

Me: We can't do two ferns because that would be derivative of *Between Two Ferns.* So, how do we all feel about three ferns?

I looked to Alex like "Can I get a vowel?" and he inched farther away. He was literally almost sitting on Paul's lap. who was still smiling so hard I thought he was about to cry.

Me: Okay, yeah, three ferns! That seems more Feng Shui.

Then, I pulled my laptop out. Because, believe it or not, I had spent months (sober) preparing for this presentation. (Actually, it would make me feel better if you didn't believe it). I opened my screen where topless photos of me littered my desktop and—pretending like everyone hadn't just seen my nipples—clicked Power Point. This is when the third exec (who'd been silent the whole time) finally spoke.

102

Third Exec: I think that's all we have time for today. Thank you.

Me: Are you sure?

Third Exec: You can email us any follow up material.

We all exchanged very messy yet businessy goodbyes. It felt like awkward post drunken sex with a stranger: embarrassing, confusing, stumbling over words while rushing out. I dropped my invisible mic as I left the building.

People always say to look at a glass half full. So, outside I said to my friends: "At least I didn't set off the fire alarm." I took their silence as agreement, because I think I'd set off a million other alarms. Ian still appeared to be having a stroke until finally he said: "That didn't go well."

The End

(Or, One Final Brain Fart)

You know that moment when you had something important to say, but can't remember what it was, or if you had anything to say at all? That's what this chapter is for: the brain farts, the farts of the brain, the diarrhea that stays in your head. It's actually more brain constipation. Like, it's in there but it just won't come out and the harder you push the more it hurts. You just have to wait it out or take something to get it out… This chapter is for the brain 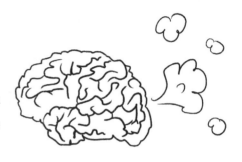 exploding realizations that will have everyone comparing me to David Sedaris: all the genius thoughts I'd hopefully remember later. Well, later is now and my only thought is of a Mark Twain quote: "It was the best of times. It was the worst of times. It was the age of wisdom. It was the age of foolishness." I'm pretty sure I read that in an Instagram model's caption once. Ok, maybe I posted it, and maybe I was wearing a bikini barely covering my nipples in the picture. I actually think a bikini picture with that caption perfectly encompasses the quote.

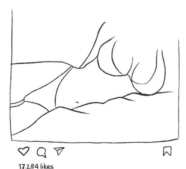

♡ ◯ ⊽　　　　　🔖

17,284 likes

It was the best of times. It was the worst of times. It was the age of wisdom. It was the age of foolishness.

If anything, I hope this book has made you incredibly confident in comparison to my shenanigans. If not, call me. I'll spice up your life (or rather create entertaining chaos I can use in my next book). This book really should be in the Self-Help section under "What Not to Do." Do not take my advice.

I did enjoy the snobbery that comes with being able to tell people *I'm writing a book*. It's like saying *I don't own a TV*, but better. Some assumed it was a picture book. Others seemed genuinely impressed. (Well, I took it as impressed. They could have been confused. Impressed and confused have kind of the same look. So, it's all up for interpretation.)

Friend: What's the book about?

Me: It's a post apocalyptic thriller.

Friend: Cool.

Me: Actually it's a memoir.

Friend: Don't take this the wrong way, but you're not famous or old enough to write one of those.

Me: Awe, thank you! Because, I look barely legal?

Friend: No, because people usually write memoirs when they're dying or after they've lived a life other people actually want to read about.

Me: Only the greats die young.

Friend: Yes, they die young, unexpectedly, having not written a memoir. Am I in your book?Me: No.

Friend: Okay, good.

This book is most likely a delayed quarter life crisis. I've actually given up on therapy and am now charging you guys to hear my thoughts. I saved the big reveal for this final chapter. This book literally was just my therapy. You're all now my therapists. You're welcome. And, if you are a therapist, you can use it as a case study for a new neurological condition. Ultimately, I wrote this when Whitney Houston developed chronic diarrhea. I took personal offense when my vet said it was from stress. After ruling out food allergies, I decided it was time for a new audience. Hopefully, you guys didn't get the same reaction Whitney Houston had to my stories.

I wrote most of this book on the toilet, where I have my best thoughts: in a constipated state most conducive to creativity. (Really honing a sexy motif.) Plus, since the internet said most people look at their phones while going to the bathroom, I figured it's best write from the audience's perspective.

My editor suggested using emojis in each chapter to appeal to Gen Z, which honestly would've probably been a better way to express my thoughts.

Maybe the next one will just be variations of ✔ 🙌 ✔ 🗿 🐓 🌷 💥 ❤ 👧 😎 👿 with illustrations of my boobs. And, I'll receive a Nobel Prize for literature under the new Emoji Category: "Her esoteric use of the eggplant is unparalleled."

My parents will call: "Can you translate this chapter? I understood up to circle eggplant car."

Me: Ugh, Daaaaad. You're so UPSIDE DOWN FACE emoji!

Dad: What?
Me: Exactly!

Full disclosure, I plan on reaching the bestseller list by twerking to each chapter on TikTok.

(Uncle Dino, I know you're reading this and watching those videos. Please don't show this to Nonna.)

Thank you for reading!

This has been....**A Very Inappropriate**
Short Story Book.

Made in the USA
Coppell, TX
02 December 2021

66985326R00066